The First Forty-Niner

Also from Westphalia Press

westphaliapress.org

The First Forty-Niner

and the Story of the
Golden Tea-Caddy

by James A.B. Scherer

WESTPHALIA PRESS
An imprint of Policy Studies Organization

Westphalia Press
An imprint of Policy Studies Organization
1527 New Hampshire Ave., NW
Washington, D.C. 20036
info@ipsonet.org

ISBN-13: 978-1-63391-101-7
ISBN-10: 1633911012
Cover design by Taillefer Long at Illuminated Stories:
www.illuminatedstories.com

Daniel Gutierrez-Sandoval, Executive Director
PSO and Westphalia Press

Rahima Schwenkbeck, Director of Marketing and Media
PSO and Westphalia Press

Updated material and comments on this edition
can be found at the Westphalia Press website:
www.westphaliapress.org

THE FIRST
FORTY-NINER

and the Story of the
Golden Tea-Caddy

By

JAMES A. B. SCHERER

Former President of the California
Institute of Technology

NEW YORK
MINTON, BALCH & COMPANY
1925

THE FIRST FORTY-NINER

Sam Brannan in His Regalia as President of the Society
of California Pioneers

TO THE

GRANDERS

Children of the Golden West

Illustrations

The First Forty-Niner

THE FIRST FORTY-
NINER

I

SAM BRANNAN, ADVEN-
turer, sailed through the Golden
Gate with his cargo of Mormons on
the last day of July, 1846. As his
ship rounded into the Bay he took in at
an eyestroke the insignificant hamlet of
Yerba Buena —San Francisco to be—
clinging like a desolate swallow's nest
to the slopes of the barren sandhills. Its
center was a wind-swept Plaza slanting
sharply down toward the Bay. Sam's
gaze focused on the flagstaff of the
Mexican custom-house, or "Old Adobe,"

on one of the upper corners of the Plaza. He could hardly believe his eyes. Instead of the flag of Mexico, the Stars and Stripes snapped in his face! He gazed a long minute, and then roared:

"*Damn—that—flag!*"

Although still in his twenties when he swapped New York for Yerba Buena, Sam was already a seasoned adventurer, and he looked the part well. Deep-chested, broad-shouldered, shaggy-headed, his extremely bland features were decorated with fashionable "side-burns and imperial," and lit up by flashing black eyes. His dress was dandified, his speech bombastic, his manners coarse, his courage and generosity bound-less. Born in Maine in 1819, he had seen America first—through buying his time at the age of seventeen from the Ohio printer to whom he had been

bound out, and becoming a literal jour-
neyman. An ambitious "literary weekly" having died on his hands in New
Orleans, his second failure occurred at
Indianapolis. Then he went to New
York and somehow became presiding
elder of the Latter-Day Saints, for
whom he published their *Messenger*. At
the time of the general exodus of the
Mormons from Nauvoo, Elder Brannan,
agreeably to instructions from his
church, chartered the little ship *Brooklyn*—370 tons burden—and filled her
with Saints, including a hundred young
ones, suitable to grow up in a new country.

So while Brigham Young led a pil-
grimage through the wilderness, Sam
sought the Promised Land by water. In
the hold of the *Brooklyn* he stowed his
printing-press, two complete flour-mills,

plows, harrows, and many such useful commodities. He rounded the Horn without serious mishap, although compelled during the long voyage to excommunicate four leaders of the party for conduct that he afterward described as wicked and licentious.

Two children were born—one a boy, named Atlantic after the ocean of his birth, and the other a girl, who for a like reason was christened Pacific.

It took six months to make the Golden Gate, including a call at Hawaii. "The Islands" were far better known to "the States" in those days than California was, being on the highroad from New York and Boston to China, while only a few stray ships ever touched on the California coast, which was on the highroad to nowhere. At the islands Sam found Commodore Stockton, with

the frigate *Congress*. Aided and abetted
by the Commodore, he there drilled his
men into a Mormon Battalion; and on
re-embarking at Honolulu he took on
board for their use "150 stand of arms,"
which might come in handy should the
Spaniards at Yerba Buena show fight.

Sam aspired to be the first American
to hoist the Stars and Stripes there, but
he rounded Telegraph Hill only to find
that Captain John B. Montgomery, of
the U. S. Sloop *Portsmouth*, had beaten
him by three weeks. That is what made
him swear. Years later, at a banquet
given in his honor by the city he vir-
tually founded, he said that on the day
of his landing Yerba Buena had but
fifty or sixty inhabitants, while his passengers and crew numbered nearly three
hundred. He further said that on sail-
ing from New York he had a faint idea

that somewhere in the mysterious West there was a port called Yerba Buena; exactly where, he did not know. He believed that a war with Mexico was imminent, and that he and his Latter-Day Saints might be interrupted by hostile cruisers. They sailed, nevertheless, and not until they landed did they feel secure. "Proud to them was that day!"

II

*W*HEN SAM DROPPED AN-
chor in Yerba Buena cove
near the sloop-of-war *Portsmouth*, the
Golden Gate had already received its
name—from John C. Frémont, an
imaginative traveler and adventurer
himself. A vision of the possibilities of
the big inland sea known to the world
for centuries as San Francisco Bay
stirred Frémont's imagination when,
standing like some second Balboa on a
Contra Costa peak, he gazed seaward
and remembered Constantinople. The
huge Bay of San Francisco, as he says
in his memoirs, is shut off from the ocean
by a mountainous wall, pierced by one

solitary gate. "To this Gate I gave the name of Chrysopylæ, or Golden Gate, for the same reasons that the harbor of Constantinople was called Chrysoceras, or Golden Horn."

Sam Brannan, tenderfoot Mormon elder, was jovially received by the handful of wayfarers that had strayed in from time to time through the Gate and occupied the crude houses surrounding the Plaza. There were but "two white ladies" in the hamlet, and the men were hard pressed for amusement. Keen on betting, their favorite sport seems to have been a mixture of horse-play and gambling. They promptly initiated Sam into their fellowship with a ceremonial described by one of them with glee. This initiation took place on the Plaza, as a matter of course—everything took place on the Plaza. Having blindfolded their victim and turned him round three times, these big overgrown boys staked bets with one another as to how long it would take Sam to get to a certain sign-post planted in the middle of the Plaza and used for the posting of notices. Behind an adobe building at the corner of Clay and Kearny streets was a slimy pool of water, created by making the adobes for the building. "Sam hesitated a moment or two, then struck a bee line for that pool, and, in less than a quarter of a minute, he was in it up to his neck!"

One can almost hear the guffaws of those lonely but jovial wayfarers, rejoicing in learning, from his good-natured behavior, that the freshly arrived Mormon elder was "one of the boys."

Yerba Buena's dull days were now

over. Social commotions crowded on one another's heels as soon as Sam Brannan landed. Some of these are set down in the quaintest of phrasing by a British bartender named Brown. With a style that suggests Tony Weller he Boswells the versatile Brannan. "The first wedding which took place after this city was under the protection of the American flag," drawls Brown, "was performed by Mr. Samuel Brannan, according to the Mormon faith. I was one of the guests, and I never enjoyed myself, at any gathering, as I did there. There was a general invitation extended to all, a large quantity of refreshments had been prepared, and every one returned to their homes, perfectly satisfied, and ready to pronounce the first wedding a grand success."

The first sermon, at least in the English language, was also achieved by Sam Brannan; "as good a sermon as any one would wish to hear," comments Brown, who adds dryly that Brannan became "well known, and will probably be remembered by many, and they will, no doubt, be surprised on hearing of his serving in this capacity."

Sam quickly fell from grace with his Mormons, who forced him to become defendant in the first jury trial ever held in Yerba Buena. The "Mormon Association" organized on shipboard charged him with misuse of funds. Through a hung jury, Sam got off. But this trial was really important. It destroyed the solidarity of the Mormons and their potential influence in the young body politic. Not only so, but the fitting of an Anglo-Saxon jury into the court of the Californian alcalde was a step of revolutionary significance. In order to meet emergencies these earliest pioneers altered at an eyestroke the institutions of centuries. One authority thinks that history provides no example more typical of the serenity and self-confidence with which Americans confronted the exigencies of their pioneer life.

Sam manages to turn up first in nearly everything. After preaching the first sermon and solemnizing the first marriage and occasioning the first jury trial in the lonesome hamlet to which he brought such exuberance, he set up and operated the first California flour-mills, secured for his family and his printing-plant a red-wood house just back of the Old Adobe, and then gave his town its first newspaper, the *California Star*.

In its initial issue his little paper promised to "eschew with the greatest

Courtesy of the California State Library

"THE OLD ADOBE" AS SAM BRANNAN FIRST SAW IT IN 1846

caution everything that tends to the propagation of sectarian dogmas," and Sam kept his promise. Indeed, none of the Mormons seemed at pains to make converts, polygamy was not in their creed, and they maintained good relations with the Gentiles. "The men were industrious, intelligent, public-spirited; the women chaste, the children well-behaved." As for loyalty, Sam's Mormon Battalion was quickly put to the test.

Its men were garrisoned not far from the Plaza, the Old Adobe being already occupied by marines from the *Portsmouth*, on guard—under a Lieutenant Watson—against expected attacks from the Spaniards. Watson, one of Brown's lodgers at the so-styled Portsmouth Hotel, gets into the bartender's story. "After Watson came ashore to guard the city," writes Brown, with his inimitable quaintness, "he made it a rule every night to fill his flask with good whisky. It was usually a very late hour when he called for it, and I would be in bed. His signal would be two raps on the shutter. As soon as I would answer he would say: 'The Spaniards are in the brush,'— this was the pass-word. I would then get up and fill his bottle, and he would leave. A short time after the arrival of whalers in port, five captains remained on shore to have a good time with some of the officers of the *Portsmouth*, Watson being one of the number. They kept me up two nights in succession, and when they finally departed, I decided to take a good night's rest. I was sleeping sounder than usual, when there were a number of raps on the window shutter. I did not hear them however, and as Watson, who had been imbibing freely, found the raps did no good, he fired off one of his pistols and sang out at the top of his voice, 'The Spaniards are in the brush!' At the barracks they began to beat the long roll. I jumped out of bed (more asleep than awake), filled Watson's flask, and was told that no one would hurt me, and to go to bed again. The Mormons had only arrived a few days prior to this event, and at the beat of the long roll they were all up and on hand with arms and ammunition, ready to furnish what service they could. There were several shots fired by those on duty, thinking they were shooting at 'Californians;' but, they found next day, to their great surprise, that instead of dead bodies, some scrub oaks had received the shots. The wind in bending the oaks hither and thither had made them suppose that 'The Spaniards' were really in the 'brush.' Watson called on me the next morning in the billiard-room, and told me that if I ever told, or even mentioned what happened the night previous, as long as I lived, I would be a dead man."

This is the only occasion on which Sam's battalion was called on to display martial valor, although Brown tells of a later call-to-arms due to the explosion of a coffee-pot in the new City Hotel! The American occupation was accomplished without any uprising of Spaniards. In fact, the Monterey alcalde, the Rev. Walter Colton, reported that the dominant emotion of the dispossessed populace was one of distressed surprise.

III

*B*ESIDES BRANNAN'S STAR
the only other California newspaper was the Monterey *Californian*,
owned and edited by Dr. Robert Semple,
who had gained fame in the Bear
Flag revolt. "Doc Semple" was so tall
that Brown had a special bed made
to accommodate him during his frequent
trips to the Bay. He came up often in
order to boom a townsite on the northern
arm of the Bay—the site of present-day
Benicia—and this caused a newspaper
feud. For Brannan had staked his own
fortunes on Yerba Buena real estate. In
fact, he now had so many irons in the
fire that he had hired a small Doctor

Jones to edit his *Star* for him, so the two medical journalists fell to—the lanky Semple and the short, rotund Jones. When they wearied of ridiculing rival land interests, each took the other's physical peculiarities for target. All of which would be ridiculous except that out of this teapot-tempest a new name was brewed for Yerba Buena—in the most absurd manner possible. Semple, an astute promoter, not without a touch of gallantry, saw that it was to his interest to compliment in every way possible the distinguished Spanish owner of his cherished townsite, General Mariano Vallejo. He also knew that the General doted on his Señora, whose first name happened to be Francisca. Semple accordingly ingratiated himself with the General by naming the city of his dreams Francisca; and at the same stroke went as far as he dared toward appropriating the name of the great Bay. Even his audacious imagination balked at the idea of "scooping" the world-famous name for a mere blue-print—if indeed he had one—and a few square miles of sand! But Yerba Buena jumped at the chance. Its alcalde, one Lieutenant Bartlett of the *Portsmouth*, had already christened the Plaza with the name of that ship, and dubbed the miry water-front Montgomery Street in honor of her captain. He now seized the advent of the new year 1847 to transmogrify Yerba Buena into San Francisco by official proclamation—but without consulting Sam Brannan.

Semple was deeply chagrined by Lieutenant Bartlett's audacity. The name Francisca, on which he had been pluming himself, became a boomerang. It so closely resembled the name San Francisco that every stranger who heard it would impute it and all his boosting of it to the impudent hamlet boomed by Brannan and Bartlett! So in sheer self-defense he had to shift to Madame Vallejo's middle name, Benicia.

An amusing reverberation of this pioneer boom-town warfare resounds through the pages of General Sherman's memoirs, written many years afterward. The man who was to prove that war is hell spent part of his youth as aide to the military governor of Monterey, where he was a warm friend of Dr. Semple. Always a partisan, Sherman never forgave San Francisco's "impudence." A stolen name, he says in his memoirs, made Yerba Buena into a city, being "convinced that this little circumstance was big with consequences. That Benicia has the best natural site for a city, I am satisfied; and had half the money and half the labor bestowed on San Francisco been expended at Benicia, we should have at this day a city of palaces on the Carquinez Straits. The name of 'San Francisco,' however, fixed the city where it now is; for every ship in 1848-'49, which cleared from any part of the world, knew the name of San Francisco Bay, but not Yerba Buena or Benicia; and, accordingly, ships consigned to California came pouring in with their contents, and were anchored in front of 'San Francisco!' "

To the cold eye of this army engineer, the steep hills encircling Yerba Buena cove loomed as obstacles, but to the ardent pioneers they seemed a challenge. These hills rose from peat quagmires, almost equally troublesome, so the pioneers simply filled up the quagmires with hilltops.

Brannan, despite his zeal as a Yerba Buena booster, was at first lukewarm toward Alcalde Bartlett's change of name. He had not been consulted about it. Perhaps Bartlett's failure to consult him was due to the fact that Sam never forgave him for presiding at that first jury trial. But the change caught the fancy of the populace, who, about this time, seized on the rotund person of Sam's small editor, Dr. Jones, and rolled him down the Plaza in a hogshead—perhaps as a communal punishment for the lukewarm spirit of the *Star*. At any rate, the paper quickly changed its date line from "Yerba Buena" to "San Francisco," which it soon began to hail as the future "Liverpool or New York of the Pacific Ocean." The *Star* kept its feet on the ground, however, urging such immediate practical necessities as a school-house, toward which Sam Brannan made the first contribution. On the upper edge of the Plaza, south of the Old Adobe, a little red school-house was built, which, during its brief but eventful career, served as a school, town-hall, court-house, tribunal of the first Vigilance Committee, church, and, finally, jail; so that it richly deserved its popular designation as The Public Institute.

Sam Brannan is the original Californiac. In due time he got out a special California edition of the *Star*, which still remains a model of its kind—written up for him by Dr. Victor Fourgeaud, freshly arrived from far-away South Carolina. With characteristic enterprise Sam sent two thousand copies of this special edition all the way to the Mississippi

Valley by pony express, to catch the eye of prospective settlers. Gold had not yet been discovered; the unenlightened States thought of California as wholly destitute of natural resources, and populated chiefly by "greasers and fleas."

IV

SAM'S FAITH IN SAN FRAN-
cisco was strengthened in the
spring of '47 by the arrival of Stevenson's Volunteers. Not since he and
his Mormons sailed in through the Gate
had anything happened to compare
in importance with the coming of a
whole regiment of New York soldiers;
despatched by the Federal government
to assist in the conquest of California
and, later, in its peaceful development.
For this twofold purpose their vessels
were loaded—according to the *Star*—
not only with muskets and rifles, but with
saw-mills and grist-mills, wagons and
plows.

Sam little foresaw that the coming of these soldiers, in which he now took so much pride, was to involve him in the most dangerous and heroic exploit of his life.

Some of the soldiers came infected with a phobia of spread-eagle patriotism. They called themselves Bowery Boys, and, until they could improvise a Tammany Hall of their own, they foregathered chiefly at "The Shades"—the first and possibly the worst of those grog-shops and gambling-hells that were to form such a feature of young San Francisco.

Here at The Shades Lieutenant Sam Roberts lost little time in organizing a local branch of a widely spread secret society styling itself The Supreme Order of the Star-Spangled Banner. Coming into the open later as the American,

or Know-Nothing political party, this parent of all ku-klux clans was now busily installing lodges throughout the States, with passwords and degrees, grips and signs, and blood-curdling oaths of secrecy. If a candidate believed in God, if he had been born in the United States, if neither he nor his wife nor his parents were members of the Roman Catholic church, he was conducted into an inner chamber "where the worthy president sate." Here the novitiate took his solemn oath of secrecy, and swore further never to vote for any man unless he were a Protestant and an American-born citizen, pledged to America for Americans. Then the passwords were revealed to him, and the grip and signals explained. You challenged a brother with the words, "What time?" He answered, "Time for work!" Second challenge:

"Are you?" Answer: "We are!" Notice of meetings was conveyed by a paper triangle; red meant danger, and brothers had to come prepared to meet it. Terrorism was their favorite weapon. When questioned about their order they always replied, "I don't know," whence the derisive name, "Know-Nothing."

Sam Brannan was always patriotic, but he was far too broad-minded for such stuff as this. Although the phrase had not yet been invented, he had "the international mind." So he took no stock whatever in the political buncombe of his fellow New Yorkers, although one may be sure he was all ears for everything they had to say. In the murky gloom of The Shades tavern they spun many a spicy yarn of their adventurous trip round the Horn. A few brought their wives with them, and the most exciting incident of the voyage had arisen from the birth of a baby.

"That child was born famous!" declaimed one of Colonel Stevenson's soldiers. "Was she not the first child ever born whose father formed part of the first expedition of armed American emigrant soldiers ever sent by their government to conquer and occupy a foreign province?"

These soldiers told with great gusto how the baby was named and christened. From her birth-ship, the *Perkins*, the news of her advent traveled over the billows to the other speeding vessels of the fleet; whereupon a convoy, the *Preble*, sailed close enough to ask for the privilege of naming her. Private Harris and his proud wife assenting, the *Preble's* captain shouted back across the water the magic name of "Alta California!"

Cheers rang over the ocean from both ships. They were destined for Alta California, and this baby was their child of destiny. The flames of their patriotism mounted higher than ever round the floating cradle of this godsend, their sign from heaven; so when all six vessels put in at Rio de Janeiro, a few days later, and found there the man-of-war *Columbia*, Colonel Stevenson resolved that the child's christening should be An Event.

His resolution stiffened on learning that the United States minister was not receiving all the deference thought to be due from an effete monarchy to the Envoy Extraordinary and Minister Plenipotentiary of the Great Republic. Colonel Stevenson not only refused to salute the Brazilian forts and to pay the customary calls of courtesy, but invited the

American minister to deliver a baptismal oration over Miss Alta California. The minister seized his opportunity. He happened to know that the Crown Prince of Brazil had been baptized in the palace at Rio by a "pompous prelate" only a few days before, so at the Sunday ceremonial on board the *Columbia* he wound up his oration with an invidious comparison between "the christening of the daughter of an American soldier" and that of " 'the royal bantling' of the Brazilian nation."

This epithet so incensed the Brazilian court that it seriously considered ordering the Americans out of port; upon hearing of which Colonel Stevenson got into his gig and was rowed from one of his vessels to another, instructing the soldiers on each ship that if they went ashore again it should be with fixed bayonets.

This so electrified his men that they jumped into the rigging and shouted cheer after cheer.

The objectionable order was fortunately not issued by the Brazilians. Although Stevenson's New York Volunteers sailed away from Rio de Janeiro without another shore leave, their already ardent jingoism had received a stimulus that was to vent itself mischievously in California, and bring them into conflict with Brannan.

Those violent disorders for which young San Francisco became notorious are usually regarded as peculiar to the place. On the contrary, they were manifestations of a national malady merely intensified by unique local conditions.

V

SAM BRANNAN'S FAITH IN California mounted to such a pitch of enthusiasm after the coming of Stevenson's soldiers that he went out into the desert to meet Brigham Young, with the resolute intention of escorting him and his pilgrims all the way to the true Promised Land. After a prolonged and arduous journey he succeeded in finding the Latter-Day Saints in the faraway Green River country, beyond Fort Hall, in what is now eastern Utah; and then turned round and marched westward with them until they reached Salt Lake Valley.

Here a dramatic episode occurred.

When Brigham Young emerged from the desert through a gap in the Uintah mountains and suddenly saw Salt Lake Valley—one of the loveliest landscapes in all the world—he stretched out his patriarchal hand and, as he stood there at the head of his people and his flocks and his herds, he uttered four syllables from which even Sam Brannan's vehement eloquence proved powerless to make him budge:

"This is the place."

Crestfallen and angry, Sam retraced his long and lonely way to California—just in the nick of time, and halted at the exact right spot. Sutter's Fort, five days up the Sacramento River from San Francisco by schooner, was a wilderness stronghold presided over by a genial Swiss captain who held title to all the land for many miles round. It was here at Captain Sutter's fort that Sam's lucky genius inspired him to stop and set up as a merchant.

This was in the fall of 1847. What ensued may best be told by his own pen:

"Captain Sutter made a contract with Marshall, Weimer and Bennett to put up a saw-mill in the fall of 1847, on the south fork of the American River, where the town of Coloma now stands (some forty miles northeast of Sutter's Fort). Having a store at the fort at that time, I agreed to furnish them with all the necessary supplies on Sutter's account, until the mill was in running order, otherwise they would not have taken the contract. On the 24th of January, 1848, when Marshall let the water into the mill-race, and the water had run clear, he picked up a piece of gold at the bottom of the race and gave it to the wife of Weimer, his partner, who was there cooking for the men, and it is still in her possession. A number of young men from the Mormon Battalion were at work on the mill for Marshall & Co., all of whom left their work and commenced washing out gold, and that was the end of the mill-building. Marshall, Weimer, Bennett and Captain Sutter claimed the right to the discovery, and charged every one who worked there ten per cent of what they found. Some of the boys became dissatisfied and went prospecting down the river for themselves, and found diggings about twenty-five miles below, on an island which has ever since been known as Mormon Island. I put up a store there, and called the place Natoma, after the name of the Indians who lived there. I also put up a store at the mill and called the place (where gold was discovered) Coloma, after the name of the tribe there."

Sam wrote this cool and carefully considered account of the discovery of gold many years after the event, in an effort to minimize a story about which he always remained sensitive. Whether "Marshall, Weimer, Bennett and Captain Sutter charged every one who worked there ten per cent of what they found" may possibly be doubted. But there is no doubt whatever as to what Sam himself did. Always a brain worker, when gold suddenly turned up he as suddenly resumed—strictly for business purposes—his Mormon authority over the horny-handed miners from his old Battalion, and took "the Lord's tithes" of all their pannings!

No less an authority than Sherman vouches for this, in his memoirs. Going up the Sacramento and American rivers with his chief, Colonel Mason, to ascertain whether gold had really been discovered, young Sherman found Sam industriously collecting tithes on Mormon Island!

One of the miners, more suspicious than the rest, approached Colonel Mason, says Sherman, and inquired whether Brannan, "as high-priest," had a legal right to take tithes. "He has a perfect right to collect them," replied the facetious Colonel—"as long as you are fools enough to pay!"

Thereafter Sam's tithe-taking ceased; but Brigham Young heard about "the Lord's money" away over in Utah, and in due time sent an apostle to collect.

"You go back and tell Brigham," rejoined Sam, "that I'll give up the Lord's

From a sketch from life by Frank Marryat

WHERE SAM TOOK TITHES FROM THE MINERS

money when he sends me a receipt signed by the Lord, and no sooner!"

That cut him off completely from the faith. A Mormon sketch of his life sadly says: "His course and habits were not consistent with the life of a Latter-Day Saint, and he was disconnected with the Church."

VI

SHERMAN AND COLONEL Mason were not the only skeptics regarding the rumor of gold. San Francisco itself refused to take the slightest interest in it until Sam came down the river and proved it, to the confusion of his own paper, the *Star*.

This was now edited by a callow youth named Kemble, one of Sam's protégés on the *Brooklyn*. Dr. Semple had moved his *Californian* up from Monterey, so that San Francisco now sported both sheets.

The first newspaper notice of the discovery was a "scoop" by Semple's *Californian* in its issue of March 15, 1848:

The First Forty-Niner

"GOLD MINE FOUND.—In the newly made race-way of the saw-mill recently erected by Captain Sutter, on the American fork, gold has been found in considerable quantities. One person brought thirty dollars worth to New Helvetia, gathered there in a short time. California, no doubt, is rich in mineral wealth; great chances here for scientific capitalists. Gold has been found in almost every part of the country."

Young Kemble promptly and persistently ridiculed his newspaper rival, denouncing the gold news so late as May 29th as "all sham—a supurb* take in, as was ever got up to guzzle the gullible."

Then a dramatic thing happened. Within a few hours of the appearance of this issue of the *Star* on the street, its

* The spelling is that of the *Star*.

[51]

owner bolted into San Francisco from the diggings, travel-stained with his long journey, and rushed through the old Plaza hatless, crying out with his bull-throated bellow:

"*Gold!* Gold! GOLD from the American River!"

Sam was thus the first herald of the stupendous discovery. As he shouted, he waved in the sunlight above his big shaggy head a flask flashing with gold-dust.

So great already was the faith in his business judgment that the whole "city" followed his lead. Skeptical San Francisco, now numbering two hundred inhabitants, followed Sam back up the Sacramento River and out its American fork as if he had been the Pied Piper. Only seven men were left in the town! Semple's paper was forced to suspend publication, with the picturesque jeremiad:

"The whole country, from San Francisco to Los Angeles and from the sea shore to the base of the Sierra Nevada, resounds with the sordid cry of *'gold!* GOLD!! GOLD!!!'* while the field is left half planted, the house half built, and everything neglected but the manufacture of shovels and pickaxes, and the means of transportation to the spot."

The *Star* itself, the very next week after having denounced the gold rumors as "sham—a supurb take in, as was ever got up to guzzle the gullible," was forced to confess that the streets of the infantile boom-town "no longer resound with the tread of stirring feet; everything wears a desolate and somber look; everywhere, all is dull, monotonous, dead."

Soon it, too, expired; all its subscribers, and even its devil, having followed Sam up the river to the diggings. San Francisco simply wiped itself off the map.

VII

SHERMAN AND MASON adopted Sam's principle, "Seeing is believing," as the best means of convincing the States. They despatched a special courier to Washington by way of the Isthmus, having first loaded him down with samples of the treasure they had collected upriver, including a tea-caddy containing 230 ounces, 15 penny-weights, and 9 grains of gold.

Sam had no need to get out any more special editions of the *Star* to attract settlers to California. With his vivid imagination he must have followed that magical tea-caddy on its enormously long journey, impatient, but fully convinced of its lode-stone qualities should it ever reach the skeptical East. Meanwhile, he profited from the influx of gold-hunters that set in from the ports of the Pacific Coast as soon as the gold news reached them, by way of Hawaii. During June and July, '48, $250,000 worth of gold-dust had come down the Sacramento River, and much of this was shipped at once to Honolulu, a kind of oceanic clearing-house. The vessels that chanced to be there having then sailed away to Portland, Mazatlan, San Blas, Guaymas, Valparaiso, and Callao, an immediate excitement resulted in those ports the like of which had never been known. In October the adventurers began to pour in through the Gate, and by New Year's Day of '49 six thousand miners were at work in the diggings, while San Francisco had become a tent city of two thousand variegated inhabitants. Sam's real estate investments were rapidly increasing in value, and he was also doing a driving business in his store at Sutter's Fort, so that he got the start of everybody else toward becoming the first California millionaire.

"The East" was so far away that although gold was discovered at Coloma on January 24th, 1848—just nine days before Mexico ignorantly ceded California to the United States—it was not until August 19th that the news appeared in any eastern paper, the New York *Herald*; and even then nobody believed it. When, on the first day of December, mail service between the two oceans was undertaken by way of the Isthmus, not half-a-dozen of the passengers on the first steamship to sail down to Chagres from New York had heard the gold rumor; and, as one of these passengers on the *Falcon* afterward said, "not one had any faith in it." But on December 5th President Polk confirmed the gold discovery in a message to Congress, Mason's courier having at last reached Washington. So instantaneous and immense was the response to the golden tea-caddy that when the *Falcon* touched at New Orleans, only one week later, she found the levees black and clamorous with gold-seekers. She had to wait there several days for General Persifer Smith, now detailed to take command of American forces on the Pacific Coast, and when she weighed anchor she was jammed to her utmost capacity by "the most excited mass of moral floodwood that ever came down the Mississippi," as one of the New York passengers declared.

The First Forty-Niner

Reaching Chagres December 28th, the *Falcon* discharged her three hundred Americans across the Isthmus to Panama City, in a journey filled with hardships and sufferings. Here they were forced to wait weeks for the belated *California,* despatched from New York several months before so as to round Cape Horn and be ready to handle the Pacific side of the "Pacific Mail's" new postal service, from the Isthmus northward.

Before the *California* reached Panama City, the golden tea-caddy had done its work so well that more than a thousand gold-seekers had joined the original *Falcon* party on the cholera-stricken Isthmus—and the little *California* had accommodations for only seventy-five! What made matters worse, the gold-fever by this time had so inflamed the west coast of South America that when the *California* did at last get up to Panama, she already carried a full passenger list of Peruvians and Chileans.* Thir-

---

* The gold fever had now reached its height on the Atlantic Coast also. Near the end of January the New York *Tribune* said: "A resident of New York, coming back after absence, would wonder at the word 'California' seen everywhere in glaring letters, and at the columns of vessels advertised in the papers about to sail for San Francisco. He would be puzzled at seeing a new class of men in the streets, in a peculiar costume—broad felt hats of a reddish brown hue, loose, rough coats reaching to the knee, and high boots. 'Californians' throng the streets; several of the hotels are almost filled with them; and though large numbers leave every day, there is no apparent diminution of their numbers . . . The ordinary course of business seems for the time to be changed; bakers keep their ovens hot day and night, turning out immense quantities of ship bread, without supplying the demand; the provision stores of all kinds are besieged by orders; manufacturers of rubber goods, rifles, pistols, bowie knives, etc., can scarcely supply the demand."

teen hundred Americans gnashed their
teeth.

These disappointed Americans were
just as ardent "patriots" as Stevenson's
New Yorkers had proved themselves to
be at Rio de Janeiro. On finding themselves deprived of their "God-given
rights" by foreigners, many of the gold-
hunters acted like madmen. They even
threatened to burn the ship whose coming they had hailed as the ark of their
deliverance. Indignation meetings re-
sounded with philippics and fiery reso-
lutions; until at last General Persifer
Smith yielded to all this clamor. He issued an utterly unwarranted proclamation bound to do harm eventually, since
it denounced all foreigners destined for
California as trespassers against the sov-
ereign rights of the United States.

The First Forty-Niner

The first results of this proclamation were merely ludicrous. Possession being nine points of the law, and the *California* being anchored a safe mile offshore, the "trespassers" simply stayed where they were. Thereupon the Americans, frantic but helpless, pounced on the ship's commander. That unlucky official, torn between duty and expediency, at last compromised his dilemma by forcing his South American passengers into berths improvised for their use on the hurricane deck, at the same time decreeing—as by a sort of divine fiat—that his vessel should carry four hundred passengers instead of the paltry seventy-five she had been built to accommodate!

A lottery was now set up ashore, with four hundred prizes; and—perhaps not unnaturally—the luck strongly favored a band of professional gamblers that had come on board the *Falcon* at New Orleans.

On the last day of January, 1849, the first steamship to sail the Pacific ocean departed for San Francisco so crowded that "it was difficult to move about in her, either on deck or in the saloons," as some of her passengers afterward declared.

During the trip up the coast she encountered two tempests, four fires, and a mutiny, in addition to running out of fuel; but on the last day of February, a San Francisco lookout descried her approach from afar, and Sam Brannan went wild with delight.

So did the whole town, for that matter. The *Alta California*, into which the two rival weekly newspapers had now merged, was just going to press as the steamship came in, and therefore carried only scant mention of the tremendous event, but eye-witnesses supply the omission. "The people ran out in joyful excitement," these say, "some going to the top of Telegraph Hill, and others to Clark's Point, the landing place. The sun was bright, the sky clear, the atmosphere quiet, the temperature warm, the Bay still, and the hills green, the beauty of the day contributing to the general happiness. At last San Francisco was bound to the Atlantic Coast by steam! So soon as the steamer could come to anchor, boats went off, and there was an anxious exchange of inquiries. The passengers, greedy to know whether the stories of the gold discoveries were true, were told that the mines were rich beyond example, yielding several millions every month, a report that could well be believed; for instead of seeing, as they expected, a harbor nearly empty and a dull village, they saw a bay crowded with ships, and a town that looked like the camp of an army."

Among the tent-dwellers they found Mexicans, Indians, Kanakas, Peruvians, Chileans, Spaniards, French, Germans, Malays, and even Chinese.

In other words, authenticated news of the gold discovery had taken so long to reach the States, and the journey of these first American argonauts was so long drawn out, that even a few Chinese gold-hunters got into San Francisco ahead of them. "But with the arrival of our steamer," as one argonaut says, "the preponderance, which thereafter grew heavier every month, was American; so that we are free to admit, that for whatever has since been done, *good* or *evil*, in

California—the Americans are essentially responsible. . . . The natural boundaries of the Bay had not at that time been encroached upon. The Bay then lifted her tides above Montgomery Street. As we walked up from the beach, we saw a succession of bleak, sandy hills, covered, here and there, with sagebrush, yerba buena ('good herb,' or mint), and a scrubby brushwood. We camped out under tents of our own construction and lived in the most rough and rude way. Salt pork and beans were the chief living. The price of a common meal was five dollars, and eggs were twelve dollars per dozen. Potatoes and eggs were brought from the Sandwich Islands. Lumber was six hundred dollars per thousand feet; and all other requirements of human life were proportionately expensive."

From a sketch from life by Frank Marryat

"THE OLD NIANTIC" AS A HOTEL IN 1849

Tacks and canvas were literally worth their weight in gold, as Sam Brannan had learned to his profit; almost all the city's new "houses" being built at this time by tacking canvas round scantlings of red-wood.

When out on the Bay at night, Sam found the effect of these transparent houses strangely fantastic—hung as they were like huge Chinese lanterns all up and down the steep hillsides engirdling the cove—giving the impression of a vast amphitheater of fire, lit up from within.

Vessels following the *California* up the coast brought from the Isthmus copies of the *Panama Star;* that quaint newspaper published by Americans left behind. Its first issue contained one sentence much too good to be lost: "If foreigners come (to California), let them till the soil and make roads, or do any other work that may suit them, and they may become prosperous; but the gold mines were preserved by nature for Americans only, who possess noble hearts."

The first number of this *Panama Star* also printed General Persifer Smith's indiscreet proclamation, soon to be flaunted openly as the banner of organized lawlessness, challenging Sam Brannan to combat.

VIII

STEVENSON'S REGIMENT, having been disbanded after the conclusion of peace with Mexico, had trooped off to the mines. But a miner's life is a hard life, so many of the Bowery Boys soon drifted back to the city, among them Lieutenant Sam Roberts, over-gifted with organizing capacity. Under his nurturing hand Tammany Hall duly bourgeoned forth into a huge tent near The Shades, and these two resorts served as rendezvous for his local chapter of patriots. They styled themselves Regulators, but, more commonly, Hounds—possibly because their main aim was to hound "greasers" and other aliens away from the preserves of noble-hearted Americans. They seized with avidity on General Smith's proclamation, and added to their numbers recruits from the streams of Americans that now steadily poured in. By the spring of '49 the Hounds had become a public nuisance in San Francisco, parading the streets in motley uniform, and helping themselves to whatever took their fancy.

Organization was the secret of their power. Washington, engrossed in the great slavery controversy, remained utterly indifferent to the welfare of the territory wrested from Mexico. For four years, therefore, California was left literally lawless; that is, without law. The Mexican laws had been wiped away, and nothing supplied to take their place. It was precisely during this period that the gold mines were inundated with a movement of men perhaps the greatest since the Crusades. Men poured in from Europe and Asia and Africa and all parts of the Americas, bringing with them "every social inheritance entailed upon humanity since the dawn of history." Their only common interest was gold fever, and of this the chief social symptom may be expressed in the homespun phrase, "Every fellow for himself, and the devil take the hindmost." So in this raw community of turmoil, where every man was a law unto himself, the only organization that really hung together and functioned was that of the Hounds, and in union is strength. There was not only no law in San Francisco, there was something far worse. The young city lay helpless in the grip of organized lawlessness. Naturally, a reign of terror resulted.

This terrorism grew with steadily increasing intensity from the spring to the midsummer of 1849. The Hounds bullied merchants by day and shot up or looted the foreign settlements by night. Their specialty was Peruvians and Chileans, possibly because these were the particular foreigners that had deprived Americans of their God-given rights on the hurricane deck of the *California*.

The climax came on Sunday night, July 15th, '49. By this time so many South Americans had come up the coast that they had their own separate quarter —Little Chile, at the foot of Telegraph Hill, where they lived mostly in tents. The Hounds, parading to an attack with fife, drums, and fiddles, swore to drive out or kill all Chileans. After much indiscriminate violence a gang entered a tent sheltering women. Having outraged a mother and her daughter, they murdered the former; but in struggling with the girl they met their match. Although wounded, she wrenched a bowie-knife from a Hound, stabbed him, and escaped with her life.

It was this outrage that roused Sam Brannan's wrath, and, under his leadership, roused the irresponsible gold-hunters to a sense of social responsibility, and their first community action. Viewed from this angle, the affair of the Hounds becomes highly significant. It was the original point of departure toward self-government, to which—let it be always remembered—California pioneers were driven by the masterly inactivity at Washington.

On the morning after the outrage,

Sam mounted a barrel at the corner of Montgomery and Clay Streets and began to harangue the passing throngs of restless gold-seekers and traders. He had just the oratorical gifts needed; deep feeling, profound courage, and a powerful, penetrating voice. His fine eyes flashing fire, his shaggy mane tossing, his utterance half-choked by emotion, with sledge-hammer eloquence he welded the throng into unity. Soon a cry rose for adjournment to the Plaza, that heart of the throbbing young city, where all vital actions began. So Sam led his buzzing swarm of hornets up the hill, and, with a sense of the dramatic that seldom forsook him, climbed on top of Alcalde Leavenworth's box of an office and used its roof as a pulpit!

This was killing birds with a vengeance. Not only could he thus proclaim truth from a housetop, but, knowing well that the alcalde himself feared the Hounds, Sam put him scornfully under his feet, and also compelled him to listen.

All San Francisco gathered round him. Soon his philippic began to take effect on the Hounds themselves, scattered here and there in the crowd. Some one called up to him to "look out!"—the Hounds had begun to move stealthily about, so as to get together, and were threatening to burn down his house.

At this time in his life, Sam loved his little home better than all his other earthly possessions. Pale with wrath, he stood for a moment quite silent, on top of the alcalde's roof; and his enemies thought him afraid. Threats were muttered; pistols appeared, with demonstrations of shooting. "Perceiving which, Sam hurled on them a torrent of his choicest invective, meanwhile baring his breast and daring them to fire," as Bancroft has it.

The effect on his listeners was magical. A thousand blazing eyes suddenly transfixed the Hounds, shrivelling their mock courage to cowardice. Seeing themselves hopelessly outnumbered, they began to slink out of sight. But Sam would not let them escape. He fought these devils with fire, the backfire of a counter-organization. Then and there, in that literally lawless place, and in an apparently lawless fashion, the argonauts paid their first tribute to Law. Under Brannan's leadership they organized into companies of hundreds, a captain over each hundred, and set out in chase of the Hounds. That same afternoon, at a second mass-meeting on the Plaza which Sam and another pioneer constrained the alcalde himself to summon, two hundred and thirty more men enrolled as emergency police, to prevent retaliation. And young San Francisco did more. Inspired once again by Sam Brannan, the roused citizens organized their first charity, making up a generous purse for pillaged and wounded Chileans. By sunset, nineteen of the Hounds, including Roberts himself, had been run down; their leader having kenneled ingloriously in the hold of the schooner *Mary*, about to weigh anchor for Stockton.

Perhaps it was from this act of Roberts that the organized and now thoroughly roused citizens got their idea of an effective prison. How ineffectual the Public Institute had become, Bartender Brown bears witness. The little red school-house, he says, "was now used as a calaboose by T. M. Leavensworth at that time Alcalda (Brown does his own spelling). One night a man, by the name of Pete, was put in the 'Calaboose,' for having cut the hair off of the tails of five horses. When asked what he did it for, he said that he wanted to send it to England, to brush the flies off the Queen's dinner-table. As Leavensworth did not send him his breakfast, he called on Leavensworth at his office, with the door of the Calaboose (to which he was chained) on his back, and told him if his breakfast was not sent up in half an hour he would take French Leave. Leavensworth sent his breakfast; but it was the first and last meal he had in that place."

Wisely discarding that place, the citi-

zens transferred Roberts from the hold
of one vessel to another—a United
States war-ship, the *Warren*, where they
lodged his pack of Hounds with him.
After they could no longer make use of
the *Warren*, they beached a deserted
brig, the *Euphemia*, and converted her
into an effectual and permanent prison.
Abandoned vessels of all kinds were now
becoming common in Yerba Buena cove,
their crews having run away to the
mines.

The procedure of Sam Brannan and
his associates was as far removed from
lynch law methods as possible. Next
day after the capture of the Hounds a
grand jury was impaneled and returned
a true bill of indictment, opening with
the charge of conspiracy "to commit
riot, rape, and murder." The prisoners
were meticulously provided with coun-

sel, having as much "legal" protection as though California had been a legally organized State instead of a totally neglected possession. Young Hall McAllister, as chief prosecutor, now began his brilliant career. Nine Hounds were found guilty, and, so far, so good. But punishment was a far different matter. McAllister says that some were for hanging, others for whipping and banishment, still others for banishment accompanied by the warning that their return would mean execution. Banishment was the final decision.

Sam Brannan gave vent to a huge disgust that these convicted criminals should be merely sent back to the States, with their ocean voyages paid for. His indignation became still more vociferous when it turned out that even this luxurious penalty could not be enforced. The Gold Rush brought many camp followers with it, including hordes of professional politicians, masters of unscrupulous intrigue. The Hounds, being themselves unscrupulous as well as thoroughly organized, and numbering some experienced ward-heelers among their adherents, managed to have their own way—their sentenced members all escaped punishment. Their organization, as such, was disbanded, but its adherents were not much disheartened. Henceforward they wrought evil by stealth instead of openly, with their hands raised against the entire law-abiding community instead of against foreigners only.

Brannan's counter-organization also disbanded, but its spirit lay dormant, waiting to be quickened again by some new, urgent need. Sam had inspired San Francisco with a social consciousness, although for a time it lay asleep.

IX

*S*AM HAD NOW BECOME THE leading citizen of an Arabian Nights city. Its growth was of that magic, incredible character that led Bayard Taylor, sent out by the New York *Tribune*, to compare it with the phantasms of oriental jugglery. Arriving in mid-August of 1849, a month after the dispersal of the Hounds, he found the harbor crowded with deserted ships, of which several had now been dragged up to the muddy water-front and converted into warehouses, to shelter cargoes dumped out on the beach. The first of these was the famous old *Niantic*, whose oak hull was pierced with a Clay street entrance above which

her enterprising owner painted the in-
gratiating sign,

REST FOR THE WEARY AND STORAGE FOR TRUNKS

Leaving for home after a stay of four
months, Bayard Taylor summed up the
changes that took place under his eyes.
"When I landed, I found a town of tents
and canvas houses, with a show of frame
buildings on one or two streets. Now I
saw an actual metropolis, displaying
street after street of well built edifices,
filled with an active and enterprising
people and exhibiting every mark of permanent commercial prosperity. Then,
the town was limited to the curve of the
bay fronting the anchorage and the bot-
toms of the hills. Now, it stretched to

the topmost heights, followed the shore around point after point, and, sending back a long arm through a gap in the hills, took hold of the Golden Gate and was building its warehouses on the open strait and almost fronting the blue horizon of the Pacific. Then, the gold-seeking sojourner lodged in muslin rooms and canvas garrets, with a philosophic lack of furniture, and ate his simple though substantial fare from pine boards. Now, lofty hotels, gaudy with verandas and balconies, were furnished with home luxury; and aristocratic restaurants presented daily their long bills of fare. Then, vessels were coming in day after day, to lie deserted and useless at their anchorage. Now scarce a day passed but some cluster of sails, bound *outward* through the Golden Gate, took their way to all corners of the Pacific."

The First Forty-Niner

By the close of '49 shipping had become so active and labor so inadequate to the demand that San Francisco actually sent its laundry to China.* Chief among Sam Brannan's commercial enterprises was the great house of Osborn and Brannan, specializing in Chinese merchandise. Foreign quarters such as Chinatown and Little Italy had got their start. A British visitor called young San Francisco "the most metropolitan port in the world."

Bayard Taylor left for home just in time to miss the seamy side of the picture, but Sherman amply supplies the deficiency. When the winter rains fell, the pioneers became fully acquainted

* This amazing statement is amply authenticated. See Ryan's "Personal Adventures in California," ii, 400, and Eldredge's "Beginnings of San Francisco," ii, 615.

From a sketch from life by Frank Marryat

THE WINTER OF '49

with the vagaries of the California climate—which, as everybody now knows, may be "unusual" when it isn't extraordinary. The winter of '49 was unusual. Rain fell in such torrents that San Francisco thoroughfares were churned into quagmires, into which loads of brushwood were hastily dumped, only to become traps for unwary men and even their horses. "Montgomery Street had been filled up with brush and clay," says General Sherman, "and I always dreaded to ride on horseback along it, because the mud was so deep that a horse's legs would become entangled in the bushes below, and the rider was likely to be thrown and drowned in the mud. I have seen mules stumble in the street, and drown in the liquid mud."

At the corner of Clay and Kearny Streets, where a more humble beast of

burden encountered a similar fate, some
wag inscribed a sign-board with the
epitaph:

"This street is impassable,
Not even jackassable."

Perhaps the weirdest sight in all this
strange city was that section of Kearny
Street where the paving, for about
seventy-five yards—between the Adams
Express office and the store of Simmons,
Hutchinson and Company—was made
up of bags of coffee-beans, sacks of fine
Chilean flour, boxes of Virginia tobacco,
cooking-stoves, and at least one piano.
The market chanced to be glutted with
such things, the streets simply had to be
paved, and no other material was available. Missteps into the mud might
prove fatal. It was not an uncommon
occurrence to see drunken men mired

to their waists. Three men got into the Montgomery Street mud one night and were suffocated before they could be rescued. Up on the sand-hills conditions were only a little better. Frail canvas houses frequently sailed away on the wings of the wind, leaving their possessors exposed to the deluge. Many men sickened and died with no better shelter than sagebrush.

But in the diggings these same dreadful rains washed showers of gold in their wake. Sam Brannan, in his store at Sutter's Fort, soon began to notice a great increase in the yield from the mines. Beginning with November, '49, the monthly output trebled what it had been in the summer. And the miners, coming down from the mountains for supplies, told Sam what had happened. Driven by the rise of the rivers away from the placers, or bars, up into the ravines, or "dry diggings," for shelter, they found there—to their very great astonishment—seams and ribs and rich pockets of gold exposed by the wash of the rains. From these dry diggings gold now poured down to San Francisco in a steadily increasing stream, stimulating trade at an almost fabulous rate as soon as the rains ceased and the streets became passable. Gold-dust had become the chief medium of exchange. Bartender Brown, with a whole regiment of white-aproned assistants behind his magnificent new bar at the Parker House, had as cash-register a huge pair of gold-scales. The freehanded miners, when paying for drinks, would hold up their buckskin pouches and let the bartenders take out a pinch with their fingers, so as to save weighing. Saloon-keepers like Brown soon learned that in this, as in all things, practice makes perfect; whence arose the test question addressed to their would-be assistants, "How much can you raise in a pinch?"

All through this welter of gold-dust and mud and champagne rings the loud voice of Sam Brannan, moving back and forth restlessly between Sacramento City —as Sutter's Fort came to be called— and young San Francisco. His activities covered the whole range of the city's wild life, from gambling to banking.

X

BY THE DECEMBER OF '49 this wildness had reached its full swing. In that month Father Taylor began his fearless preaching from the porch of the Old Adobe, and a letter he received preserves the scene. "It was on a Sunday morning in December," writes his admirer, "when, landing from the Panama steamer, I wended my way with the throng to Portsmouth Square. Three sides of the square were occupied by buildings which served the double purpose of hotels and gambling houses, the latter being regarded as a very reputable profession. On the fourth and upper side of the square was an adobe building, from the steps of which you were discoursing from the text, 'The way of the transgressor is hard.' It was a scene I shall never forget. On all sides were gambling houses, each with its band of music in full blast. Crowds were going in and out; fortunes were being lost and won, terrible imprecations and blasphemies rose amid the horrid wail, and it seemed to me that Pandemonium was let loose."

But an experience of Parson Williams, another of the early preachers, suggests the other side of this picture. One of the first forty-niners to bring his family to California with him entered the Parson's little church one Sunday morning accompanied by his wife and baby. During the sermon the child cried, and the mother was about to go out; but the wise preacher asked her to stay, saying that the sound of her baby's voice would speak to the hearts of men whose own wives and children were far away much more eloquently than any words of his. "Never shall I forget," says a visitor, "the sobs and tears which these words evoked throughout that rough assembly. That infant's cry seemed to them the music of angels."

From the second-story windows of the *Alta California's* new building on Washington Street, Sam Brannan could now look out on a plaza miraculously different from that lonely playground of the overgrown boys that had welcomed him on his arrival. He saw beneath him a variegated bazaar of all nations, crowded into a single small square: turbaned Turks and Hindus; tattooed New Zealanders; jet-black Abyssinians; fiery-eyed Malays with their short, sickle-shaped swords; swarthy but handsome Kanakas; pig-tailed Chinese in blue smocks and huge basket-hats; a few even of the hermit Japanese; fur-muffled Russians, cheek-by-jowl with shivering, half-naked Indians; Irish, their shillalahs ever ready; Frenchmen smoking little black pipes, and "Dutch Charlies" puffing at enormous meerschaums; Englishmen, with and without their aitches; dark-visaged Italians; Spanish of all kinds, from grandee to *vaquero*, outnumbered only by Americans, each of them a walking arsenal. Native Spaniards furnished the high lights of this ever-shifting kaleidoscope —gorgeous in velvet jackets and snowy ruffles, plush trousers slit up at the sides, and long, gaudy *serapes* trailing to their silver-spurred heels. Occasionally some gayly dressed woman, jealously escorted, would catch Sam's attention on the edge of the crowd. Never before had there been such a city, composed so exclusively of men, and of men exclusively young—"such men as enlist in the first years of a war." Bret Harte's biographer says that a man of fifty was pointed out as a curiosity as he pushed his way through this throng. Sam Brannan, just turned of thirty, now belonged to the elders of the city.

The coarse gold of his singular character was tried to its highest values by fire. On the Christmas eve of '49 the first of the Six Great Fires devastated young San Francisco. The center of desolation was the Plaza. It was now faced from the Bay by the Eldorado gambling-saloon, the Parker House, Denison's Exchange, and the United States Coffee House—"forming, collectively, the rendezvous of the city, where everybody could be found at some time of the day"—and these buildings all disappeared. But by the end of three days all rubbish had been cleared away, and the frames of several buildings put up. San Francisco worked with such feverish energy that a man wrote home to his folks that they must pardon his spelling, as he lacked the time to dot his i's or cross his t's. In three weeks all the burnt buildings were replaced by new ones, of better construction. This was the gamblers' fire, costing them a round million. Bartender Brown speaks a good word for the mud. "It was in the street a foot thick," he says, "and it was a good thing. After a hard fight with water and mud, thrown by scoops and shovels against the buildings, the fire was stopped."

May 4th, 1850, the merchants' fire broke out, and swept away three entire blocks of shops and warehouses, with a loss of four millions. June 14th a third conflagration wiped out the district bounded by Clay and California Streets, Kearny Street and the water-front. September 17th, the fourth fire in less than one year destroyed a hundred and twenty-five buildings; and worse was to follow.

May 4th, 1851—the anniversary of the merchants' fire—"*the* great fire" occurred. Three-quarters of the city disappeared in ten hours, the loss being at the rate of a million an hour.

But this was an indestructible city. On what had been the streets, men such as Sam Brannan said, "Well, the bay is still here, and the people are here, and the mines are still left!" So Sam and

his associates went to work and built a
new city, richer, stronger than before.
In far-away Germany the slogan of San
Francisco was reported to be, "Go ahead,
young California, who the hell cares for
a fire!" The town chose the phœnix as
its seal.

This fifth and greatest fire having occurred on the anniversary of the second
one, public opinion, led again by Sam
Brannan, charged it to the infamous
gang still infesting San Francisco, and
"wicked enough to do this or any other
heinous thing." Sam's belief was cor-
roborated by the discovery of enormous
loot in dives occupied by hordes of
"Sydney coves," or "Sydney ducks," that
had poured in from the convict settlements of Australia as abettors in crime to
the Hounds.

Sam now roused the slumbering social

spirit that his courage had originally called into being. And the evolving social order advanced to a new stage. Organization shaped itself this time into a "Night Patrol," duly authorized by city ordinance. The first mayor, John W. Geary, swore the volunteers in, and the city marshal directed their work.

This was the real beginning of the celebrated Vigilance Committees, whose story has so often been told. On June 9th, 1851, the first Vigilance Committee was organized in Sam Brannan's office. He was its first president, and its first spokesman before the San Francisco public, at a time when it urgently needed defenders. This was the greatest work of his life.

In scenes of wild turbulence, the first Vigilance Committee demonstrated its power when it was but two days old. It did so by hanging John Jenkins, a giant Australian, for the theft of a safe from Long Wharf in broad daylight—so bold had the robbers become. His pals having failed in their efforts to rescue him, Jenkins was swung in the moonlight from the south gable of the Old Adobe, Sam Brannan seizing the rope with the loud cry:

"Every lover of liberty and good order lay hold!"

Revenge came on June 22nd in the guise of "the poor man's fire." This laid waste sixteen blocks of the more humble dwellings, and caused a loss of three millions. The Old Adobe was also burnt, as if to avenge Jenkins, and so was Sam's precious house. The *Alta California* building went with them. Printed next day from borrowed type on borrowed presses, the big newspaper feelingly said, "Thousands of people are homeless. We are sick with what we have seen and felt, and need not say any more." Many citizens gave up in despair, and no wonder—San Francisco had been in ashes six times in a year and a half.

But this proved to be the last of the Six Great Fires, the last flare of the red torch of destruction. Sam's Vigilantes saw to that. By the end of the month they numbered between five and six hundred members, and a decrease in crimes of all kinds ensued.

Sam led in the work of incessant rebuilding, and each time he saw the city grow stronger. Makeshift storeships such as the old *Niantic* were succeeded by large fireproof warehouses, Sam actually importing dressed granite for that purpose from China. Other fireproof materials included lava from Honolulu, and bricks from Australia, New York, and even London.

The chief result occasioned by the fire-fiends in their conflict with Brannan was the San Francisco Committee of Vigilance, consisting as it did of men wholly abandoned by their government, but determined at all costs to establish law in a literally lawless community, to set up and maintain social order against organized destruction intrenched in political corruption. Bancroft, who is seldom fair to Brannan, feels called on to say, "Peculiar as he was in some respects, I cannot but regard his connection with the first Vigilance Committee as the brightest epoch of his eventful life; and so long as society holds its course in San Francisco, his name should be held in honored and grateful remem-

brance. With the most cheerful reck-
lessness he threw his life and wealth
into the scale; anything and everything
he possessed was at the disposal of the
Committee, free."

"Free" is perhaps as good a single
word as any with which to sum up Sam
Brannan. It suggests both his strength
and his weakness. He was *too* free—an
utter stranger to discipline self-applied,
and too impatient to apply it temper-
ately and consistently to others. Hence
a sober-minded young merchant, William T. Coleman, who had balked Sam's
dangerous impetuousness in an earlier
crisis, now took the reins out of Sam's
hands and became San Francisco's actual
law-giver, hundreds of good men assist-
ing him. That strange martyr to civic
righteousness, James King of William,
was indeed to seal the good cause with

his blood. In the achievements of such men as these Sam had no part. He could only do his own work, not theirs. He had the defects of his qualities to an outrageously abundant degree. But his qualities—these he had in superlative measure. These prudent ones, when he had aroused public sentiment, took the reins out of his hands, and drove straight. Without their direction, Sam's initiative would have run wild. But he did initiate. His virtue is that he started things—never counting the cost to himself.

XI

SAM'S EARLY VIGOR WAS SO
great that it needed more than one
lusty city to feed on, and this surplus
energy found its vent at Sacramento.
Formerly a mere *embarcadero*, or land-
ing-place, for Sutter's Fort, this new
river-town vied for a while with San
Francisco itself in growth, being the
gate to the northern gold regions not
only for immigrants by way of the sea,
but for those of the overland trails too.
In '49 nearly forty thousand immigrants
reached California by sea, with at least
an equal number overland, so that the
state's population at the close of the year
amounted to a hundred thousand. Prac-

tically all of these hundred thousand people paid tribute to Sacramento City at one time or another. Sam, having been on the ground there since the autumn of '47, and having completely superseded the easy-going Captain Sutter as master of the local situation, presently owned a fourth of Sacramento City, where his store drove a business of $150,000 a month. Always lavishly generous, he celebrated the opening of his "City Hotel" by entertaining the entire populace for a day, at a stupendous cost for "refreshments." Asked to name the streets of the town that was to become California's capital, he began by proposing to call its main thoroughfare after Sherman, but that rigid young soldier objected, substituting the A, B, C-1, 2, 3 plan that prevailed.

In San Francisco itself, Brannan, in

the earlier 'fifties, owned one-fifth of the city, including nearly all the property abutting on Market Street. Land values being simply fabulous, his rents alone would have made him the first California millionaire. "I was forced to believe many things," says Bayard Taylor, "which I was almost afraid to write. The Parker House rented for $110,000 yearly, at least $60,000 of which was paid by gamblers. A citizen died insolvent to the amount of $41,000. His administrators were delayed in settling his affairs, and his real estate advanced so rapidly in value meantime, that after his debts were paid his heirs had a yearly income of $40,000. These facts were indubitably attested; yet hearing them talked of as matters of course, one could not help feeling as if he had been eating of 'the insane root.'" Interest charges

From a sketch from life by Frank Marryat

THE BAR OF A GAMBLING SALOON

at one time reached the rate of ten per cent a month; and San Franciscans indeed crowded into a month the full life of a year.

The first general results of the gold discovery have been summarized as a vast increase in wealth, unexampled industrial production and commercial activity, and a condition of constant excitement that has contributed to form the intellectual character of Californians. It would be impossible to find a more typical, all-round representative of this wild Midas era than Sam Brannan, compounded of its virtues and vices, and always in the thick of the maelstrom.

He was prime mover in nearly every early enterprise, whether for profit or philanthropy. His generosities ranged from street beggars to the ambitious

Music Fund, which honored him as its principal patron. He helped to organize the Society of California Pioneers in 1850; and, upon its reorganization, three years later, became president, with W. T. Sherman as treasurer. He played a major part in the great fire companies that were necessitated by wholesale arson, and that exerted a unique effect socially. To the Brannan Fire Association he gave the best fire-engine of its time. He was a member of the first city council, and later became a state senator. Nobody held richer or bolder revels, or lavished more money on the beautiful Lola Montez. He contrived often to visit New York, always with his weather eye open; borrowing at three per cent there instead of paying usury in San Francisco. When all his business associates still sneered at the "cow counties" south of the Tehachepi Mountains, Sam staked his faith on southern California to the extent of purchasing 160,000 acres of land in Los Angeles county, which was thus ultimately thrown open to settlement by small farmers. His horizon knew no bounds; he had indeed the international mind. He not only traded across the Pacific with China and Hawaii—owning large properties in Honolulu—but crossed the Atlantic several times, bringing back from Europe blooded stock and choice grapes for the benefit of his golden state. And he flashed his beneficence southward; Mexican patriots enjoyed his support in throwing off the yoke of Maximilian. With California gold he floated their huge bond issue for them, and the American legion down there was known as Brannan's Contingent, since Sam paid the bills. He was spot-light man of his mad and magical city. When the paint-brush of advertising followed the flag, stage-coach travelers were greeted everywhere with huge, staring signs: *"Try Tono, Buy Bungay*—SAM BRANNAN BUYS IT!" Tribute could go no further.

XII

SAM WAS PART AND PARCEL
of the most fascinating city on
earth for half his lifetime, and one of
its star performers until 1859. In that
year a boom-town turned his luck. He
bought an immense tract of land in
Napa Valley, to the north of San Francisco Bay, in order to exploit the hot
springs there. "The Saratoga of California" now became his dream, and he
welded the two names into one: Calistoga. He poured out his thousands and
tens of thousands into Napa Valley,
which proved to be his bottomless pit.
Of all his investments, the only thing
that paid there was his distillery, and its

output stole away his brains. In San Francisco it presently became a street saying that he was seldom ever sober after noon.

His friends, like his fortune, now fell away. His wife divorced him, taking their four children to Germany. With prodigal and characteristic liberality he settled on her an allowance that practically exhausted his resources.

His old bravado died hard. An ardent Union man, he achieved the front page in New York newspapers during the Civil War through a fracas with a slave-captain in the St. Nicholas Hotel, and then made all San Francisco guffaw with an over-costly celebration of the downfall of Charleston, which had not yet fallen. He braved a gang of midnight marauders on his Calistoga estate, and took eight successive bullets into his rum-soaked carcass without flinching.

In a lone spectacular outburst of his more advanced years he attempted the retrieval of his fortunes. From an almost forgotten bank-vault in New York City he took out his musty Mexican bonds—those he had validated years before with hard cash—and went down to the now triumphant republic, apparently ignorant of the adage that associates republics with ingratitude. But the Mexicans seemed to listen to his claims. In return for past favors Sam received a land-grant of some two million acres, and wrote letters home boasting of fifty consecutive days in the saddle, riding through his domain.

He was then more than sixty years old. Returning to the States, once more he "electrified" New York and San

Francisco with grandiose schemes of colonization. But it chanced that the Yaqui Indians, who had squatted on Sam's two million acres from times immemorial, had notions of their own about colonists—and Sam was unable to "come back."

In his deserted old age he married a Mexican woman and loafed like a *péon* around a little ranch in San Diego county, just above the Mexican border; bloated with drink, his right side paralyzed from dissipation. Once he got back to San Francisco, now become that city of palaces of which he had so often dreamed. He lodged in a two-bit rooming house, and was interviewed by a reporter as a sort of curious antique. He told this reporter that two men who had just crossed the street to avoid him were men he had set up in business. Then he slouched back to his little God-forsaken ranch in the south—and, behold, on a sudden, the miracle! Mexico actually paid him $49,000, a meager enough interest on his huge loan; but that was not the miracle. Sam Brannan, renegade adventurer—drunkard, spendthrift, rake—Sam took every dollar of that money and paid his debts with it, quit drinking, got rid of his paralysis, and died, on the rounding of his seventieth milestone, redeemed through the power of his will.

He died in the city of San Diego, May 14th, 1889. For want of money to bury him, his body lay in a receiving vault more than a year. One Alexander Bledon finally bought six feet of earth in Mount Hope Cemetery, and had him decently buried—in division 4, section 2, lot 7. At last accounts a two-inch stake marked his grave. An obscure San Francisco street bears his name.

There are so many morals to this tale of the First Forty-Niner that each reader may be left to choose his own.

POSTSCRIPT

POSTSCRIPT

To-day a beautiful monument to Robert Louis Stevenson distinguishes the old San Francisco Plaza, renamed Portsmouth Square and completely surrounded by Chinatown. It used to be Stevenson's loafing-place. Here he would lie prone in the sun, gossiping with truants and loafers from all the Seven Seas as he burnished the lamp of his fancy. "Of all romantic places for a boy to loiter in," thinks Stevenson, "that Chinese quarter is the most romantic. There, on a half-holiday, three doors from home, he may visit an actual foreign land, foreign in people, language, things and customs. The very

[121]

barber of the 'Arabian Nights' shall be at work before him, shaving heads; he shall see Aladdin playing on the streets."

More than thirty years after Sam Brannan had cursed the flag that flew over this Plaza, "R. L. S." crossed the plains to San Francisco; and, looking back through three decades of marvelous history, christened it The City of Gold —"that City of Gold to which adventurers congregated out of all the winds of heaven. I wonder," he exclaims, "what enchantment of the 'Arabian Nights' can have equalled this evocation of a roaring city, in a few years of a man's life, from the marshes and the blowing sand!"

Stevenson was not the first rover to be struck with the sheer wizardry of young San Francisco. A French gold-hunter, Edmond Auger, seeing it for himself in

'49, compared "this marvelous city, bazaar of all the nations of the globe," with "the fantastic creations of 'The Thousand and One Nights.'" And Bayard Taylor, in that same magical year, went so far as to predict that "of all the marvelous phases of the Present, San Francisco will most tax the belief of the Future. Its parallel was never known, and shall never be beheld again. I speak only of what I saw with my own eyes. Like the magic seed of the Indian juggler, which grew, blossomed and bore fruit before the eyes of his spectators, San Francisco seemed to have accomplished in a day the growth of half a century."

So this little book is a story of gold and the magic of gold—of the magical birth of a city, and of the almost equally incredible career of one of those hardy adventurers who wrought the Golden Age of California. There was never another golden age like it. In the early mining camps—such camps as Hangtown and Hell's Delight, Yuba Dam, Dead Man's Gulch, and Gouge-Eye—the miners used to sit around the fires at night and recount the thrills of the day: comparing their pannings, telling of grizzly bears seen or slain, and sometimes reporting "coarse gold." Without knowing it, they belonged to an age of coarse gold: primitive, raw, unrefined, but dramatic, heroic, Homeric. As a British observer expressed it, "the coarse, the horny-handed, the bull-throated—they set the fashion, these men of the pickaxe and pistol, and a fine fire-eating fashion it was!"

Sam Brannan, the First Forty-Niner, was, in two words, coarse gold.

Postscript

Readers unfamiliar with the unique significance of San Francisco's earliest years may gather it at a glance from a few striking sentences in Professor Josiah Royce's "study of American character," as he describes his volume on California in the American Commonwealths series. "California," says this Harvard philosopher, "was to be morally and socially tried as no other American community ever has been tried, and was to show as we Americans have not elsewhere so completely and in so narrow compass shown both the true nobility and the true weakness of our national character. All our brutal passions were here to have full sweep, and all our moral strength, all our courage, our patience, our docility, and our social skill were to contend with these our passions. Early California history is not for babes,

nor for sentimentalists; but its manly
wickedness is full of the strength that,
on occasion, freely converts itself into
an admirable moral heroism. . . . In
San Francisco the great battle was to be
fought and the victory won, for the
cause of lasting progress in California.
Upon the city by the Golden Gate all
the permanent success of the good cause
depended. Here the young State was, so
to speak, nourished. Here the ships and
a great part of the immigrants came.
Here was from the first the centre of the
State's mental life, and to a great extent
of its political life. Here good order
must be preserved, if any permanent order was to be possible elsewhere. And
so the progress of San Francisco was to
be identical with the progress of the
whole of the new State."

Postscript

The writer is indebted to **Mr. Robert E. Cowan** not only for his excellent bibliography of California, but also for his personal kindness in reading this manuscript for errors of fact. And no courtesy could possibly exceed that of the officials of the State Library at Sacramento in making available their rich stores of original material.

JAMES A. B. SCHERER.

San Francisco, California,
September 9, 1925
California's Diamond Jubilee.